MASTERWORK CLASSICS

COMPILED AND EDITED BY JANE MAGRATH

MW01040309

CONTENTS

May be used with *Alfred's Basic Piano Library* as early as Lesson Book 5.

Start *Masterwork Classics 5* after page 20 in Lesson Book 5.

Second Edition
Copyright © MCMXCVII by Alfred Publishing Co., Inc.
All rights reserved. Printed in USA.

Cover art: Planet Art

THE MUSIC

Compositions in *Masterwork Classics* are among the best literature available at this level by the standard composers. The music was chosen because of its quality, the concepts that can be taught from the pieces and the uniqueness of the repertoire to the teaching literature. Pieces included will develop the energetic and exuberant side of playing, as well as the more reflective and lyrical aspects of pianism. Some pieces are familiar favorites while others, though seldom heard, are sure to become favorites with students and teachers alike. Recital and contest groupings can be put together with ease from these volumes.

THE SEQUENCING

A suggested order of study for the pieces is provided on the next page. The repertoire was chosen and placed in a specific order to allow technical and musical principles found in the pieces to build on one another sequentially as the student progresses through the volume. While most students will want to play all or most of the pieces in this book, some students will be able to progress more rapidly. In that case, the teacher should elect to teach those pieces which allow the student to build aspects of his/her playing enabling them to move to a higher musical and technical level.

CORRELATION WITH ALFRED'S BASIC PIANO LIBRARY

The volumes in *Masterwork Classics* are loosely correlated with Alfred's Basic Piano Library so that students can have the advantage of playing music of the classical masters while gaining solid fundamentals of pianism through the method. Most students who have begun *Lesson Book 5* will be able to play, with ease, pieces from *Masterwork Classics 5* after they have reached approximately page 20 of *Lesson Book 5*. Teachers using any teaching method can also use these books to pace the student's growth through the classical literature.

PRACTICE AND PERFORMANCE

Books to supplement the *Masterwork Classics* volumes are available for each volume. *Practice and Performance* are guides for the student to help him/her learn about the form, character and patterns in the pieces, as well as how to practice each piece more efficiently. *Practice and Performance* contains a practice guide for each piece from the corresponding volume of *Masterwork Classics*. Help is given the student in terms of how to practice a piece in three stages:

> GETTING READY TO PLAY—preparation
> PRACTICING FOR PERFORMANCE—playing
> FINISHING FOR PERFORMANCE—listening and evaluating what was heard,
>   then reworking.

"Notes to the teacher" accompany the practice guide for each piece. When lesson time is limited, the series *Practice and Performance* can aid the teacher by effectively organizing student practice techniques. These practice guides are appropriate for piano students of all ages and can provide substantial help in establishing ways to practice, in addition to building expectations for accomplishment.

EDITORIAL PRINCIPLES

All literature in this book is drawn from the library of high-quality standard editions by Alfred Publishing Company. As always, the highest editorial practices have been maintained in the compilation and editing of these works. Occasional fingerings, articulation markings and sparse dynamic markings have been added. These few editorial suggestions assist the teacher and student in rendering a stylistic performance of a work.

Heartfelt appreciation is extended to Morty and Iris Manus, Willard Palmer and Maurice Hinson for their high editorial principles, for their scholarship and for allowing the creation of this volume.

This order of study is suggested to allow playing requirements for each piece to build upon skills developed in earlier repertoire in *Masterwork Classics 5.*

Literature is listed in two columns, since most students will study at least two pieces from this book simultaneously. This dual list allows contrast of styles for the student.

March in D Major

BWV Anh. 122

from the *Notebook for
Anna Magdalena Bach*
(1725)

Menuet in D Minor

BWV Anh. 132

from the *Notebook for
Anna Magdalena Bach*
(1725)

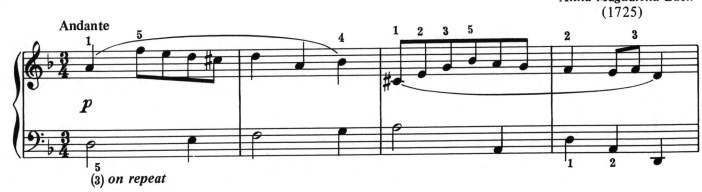

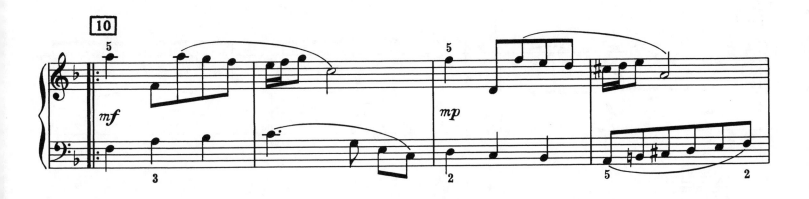

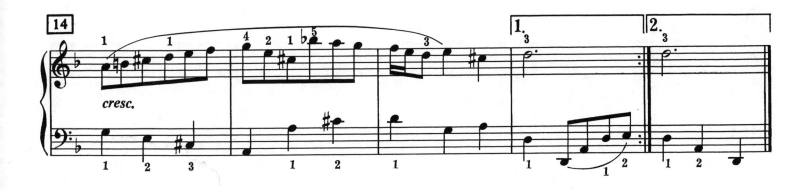

Prelude in G Major

Johann Kuhnau
(1660 - 1722)

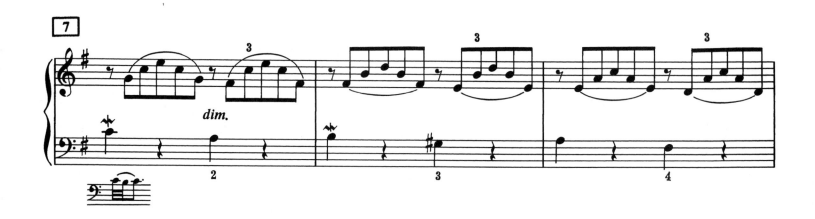

Prelude in F Major

BWV 927

J. S. Bach
(1685-1750)

Sonatina in C Major

Op. 157, No. 4

Allegro moderato

Fritz Spindler
(1817 - 1905)

Sonatina in F Major

Anh. 5, No. 2

Ludwig van Beethoven
(1770 - 1827)

Sonatina in C Major

Op. 39, No. 3

Frank Lynes
(1858 - 1913)

13

Sonatina in G Major

Op. 36, No. 2

Muzio Clementi
(1752-1832)

Sonatina in F Major

Op. 168, No. 1

Anton Diabelli
(1781 - 1858)

Sonatina in C Major

Op. 168, No. 3

Anton Diabelli
(1781 - 1858)

(a) Here the small note is played on the beat and receives its written value:

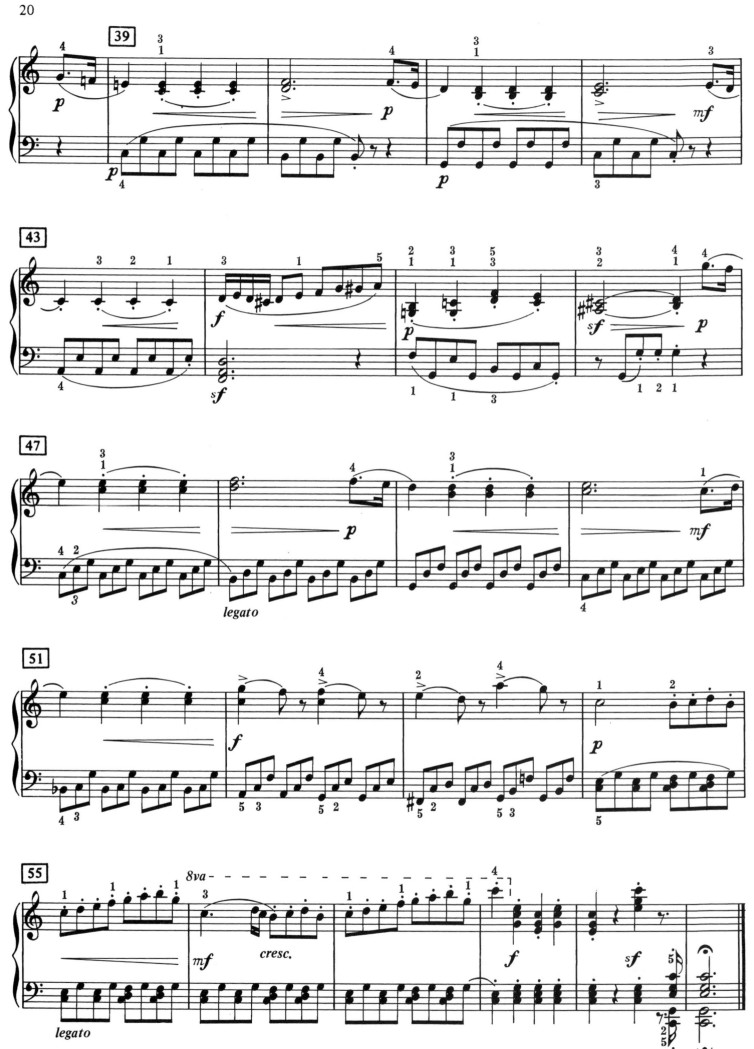

A Sad Story

Op. 63, No. 12

J. L. Streabbog
(J.L. Gobbaerts)
(1835 - 1886)

Ave Maria

Op. 100, No. 19

Johann Friedrich Burgmüller
(1806 - 1874)

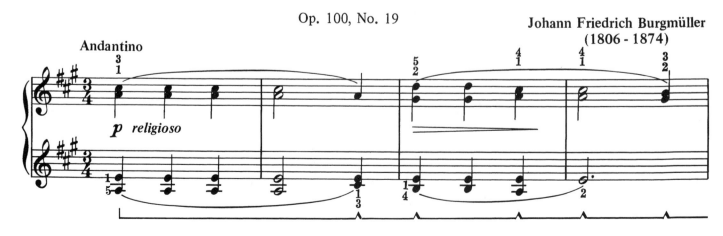

Angels' Voices

Op. 100, No. 21

Johann Friedrich Burgmüller
(1806 - 1874)

Will-o-the-Wisp

Op. 140, No. 15

Cornelius Gurlitt
(1820 - 1901)

The Cadets

Op. 64, No. 11

J. L. Streabbog
(J.L. Gobbaerts)
(1835 - 1886)

The Orphan

Op. 64, No. 4

J. L. Streabbog
(J.L. Gobbaerts)
(1835 - 1886)

Etude in C Major

Op. 47, No. 1

Stephen Heller
(1813 - 1888)

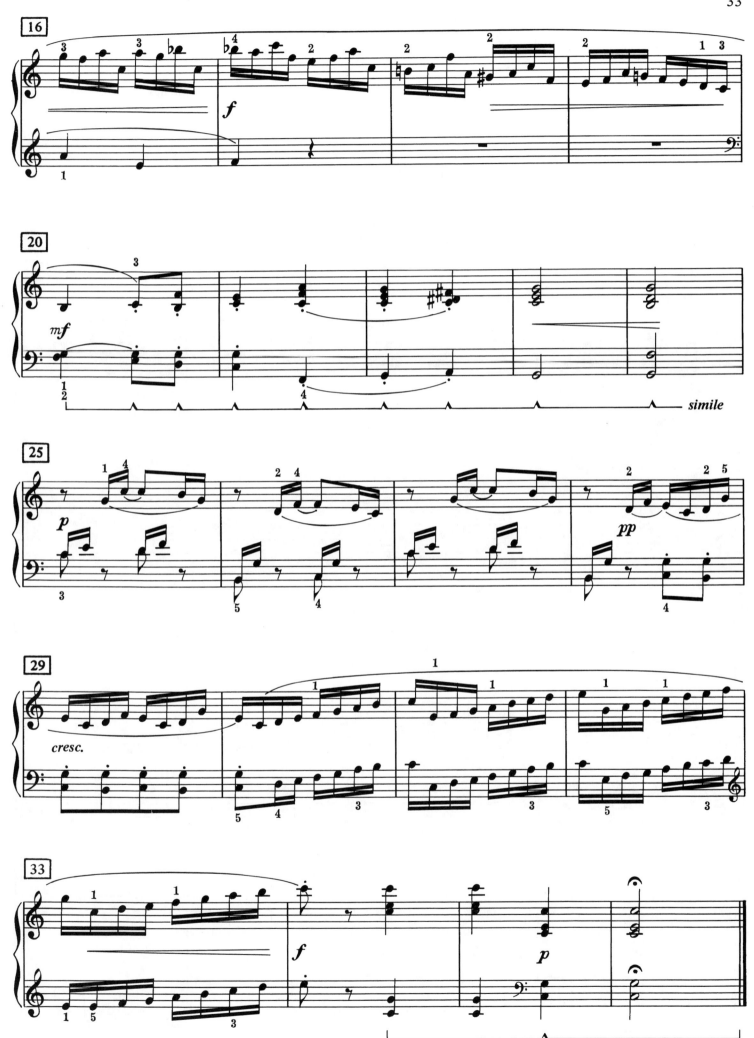

The Farewell

Op. 100, No. 12

Johann Friedrich Burgmüller
(1806 - 1874)

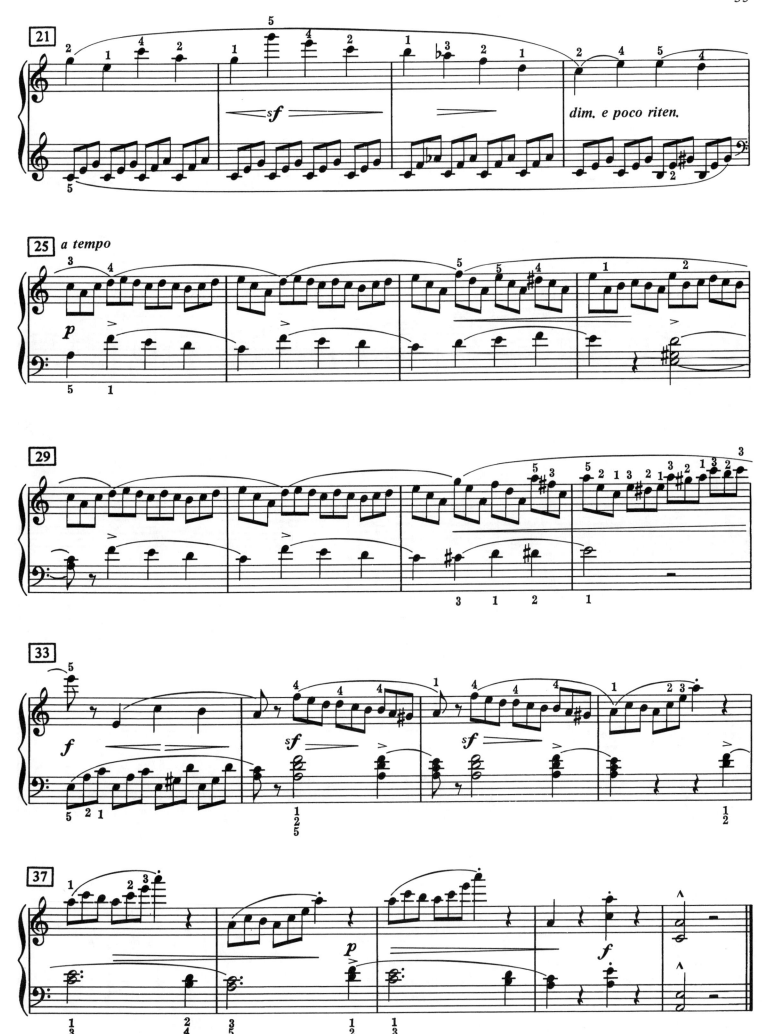

Scherzo in D Minor

Cornelius Gurlitt
(1820 - 1901)

con pedale

In a Woodland Glade

Op. 98, No. 6

Alexander Gretechaninoff
(1864 - 1956)

Rocking

Op. 31, No. 7

Vladimir Rebikov
(1866 - 1920)

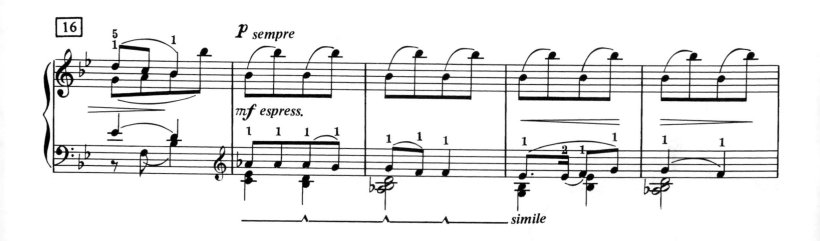

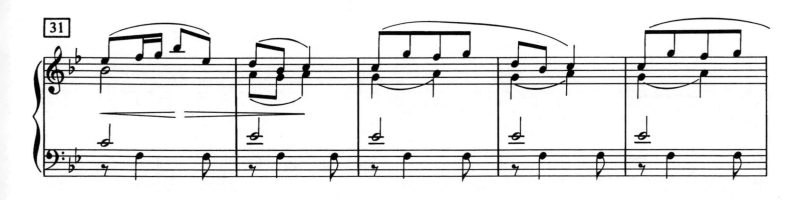

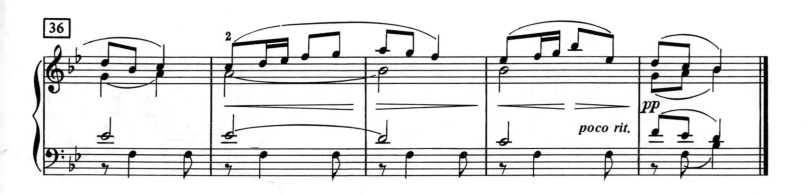

Andantino

Aram Khachaturian
(1903 - 1978)

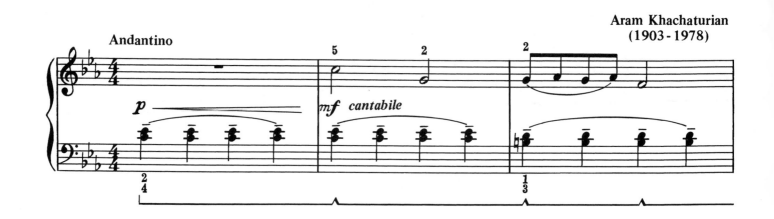

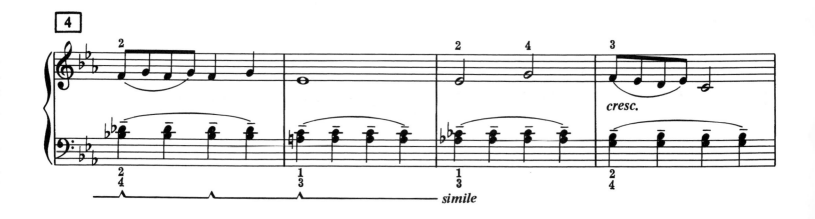

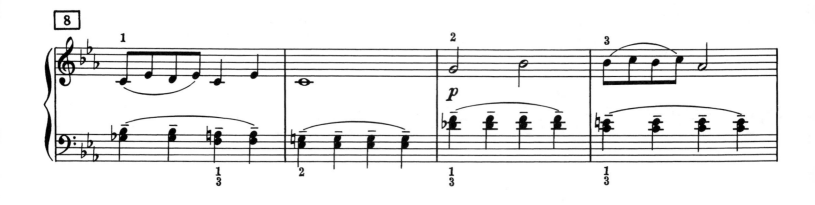

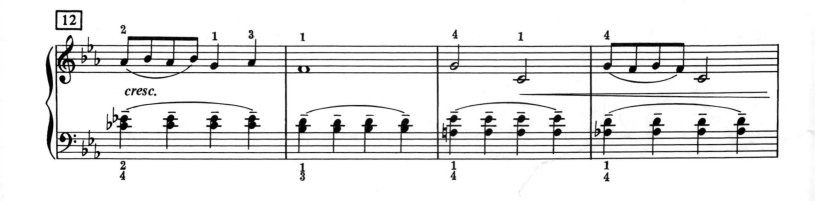

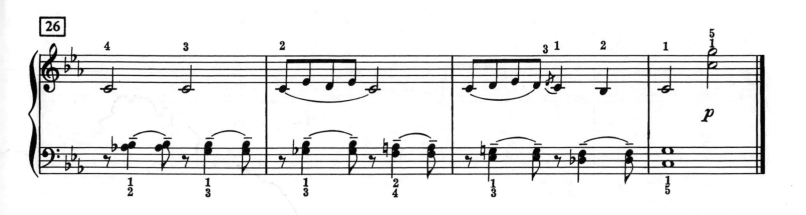

The Bandit

Béla Bartók
(1881 - 1945)

The Village Girls

Béla Bartók
(1881 - 1945)

Etude in A Minor
Op. 27, No. 3

Dimitri Kabalevsky
(1904 - 1987)

Allegro vivace

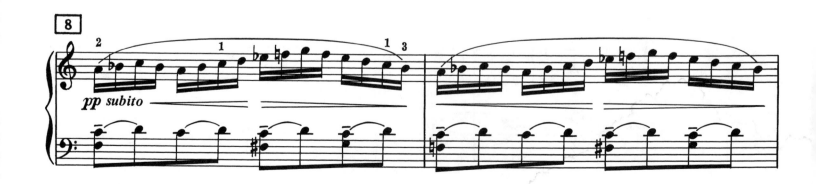

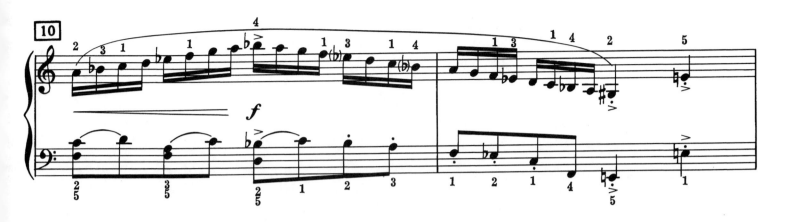

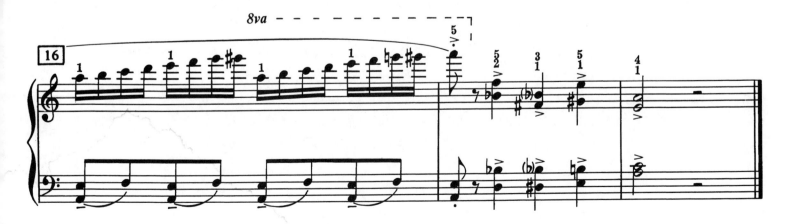